WOULD YOU REALLY RATHER DIE THAN GIVE A TALK?

THE COMIC-BOOK GUIDE TO BRILLIANTLY SURVIVING YOUR NEXT BUSINESS PRESENTATION!

MICHAEL EGAN

AMACOM

American Management Association

New York • Atlanta • Boston • Chicago • Kansas City • San Francisco • Washington, D.C.
Brussels • Mexico City • Tokyo • Toronto

This publication is designed to provide accurate and authoritative
information in regard to the subject matter covered. It is sold with
the understanding that the publisher is not engaged in rendering
legal, accounting, or other professional service. If legal advice or
other expert assistance is required, the services of a competent
professional person should be sought.

Library of Congress Cataloging-in-Publication Data

Egan, Michael
    Would you really rather die than give a talk?: the comic-book
    guide to brilliantly surviving your next business presentation /
    Michael Egan.
        p. cm.
    Includes index.
    ISBN 0-8144-7941-3
    1. Business presentations. I. Title
    HF5718.22.E35 1997
    658.4'52–dc21   97-23151
                                                                   CIP

Printing number

10 9 8 7 6 5 4 3 2 1

THIS INSCRIPTION WAS FOUND ON THE WALL OF AN EGYPTIAN TOMB DATING BACK MORE THAN 3,500 YEARS!
IT TRANSLATES: *BECOME THEREFORE A MIGHTY CRAFTSMAN IN THY SPEECH, FOR THEREBY SHALT THOU GAIN IN LIFE THE VICTORY.*

CONTENTS

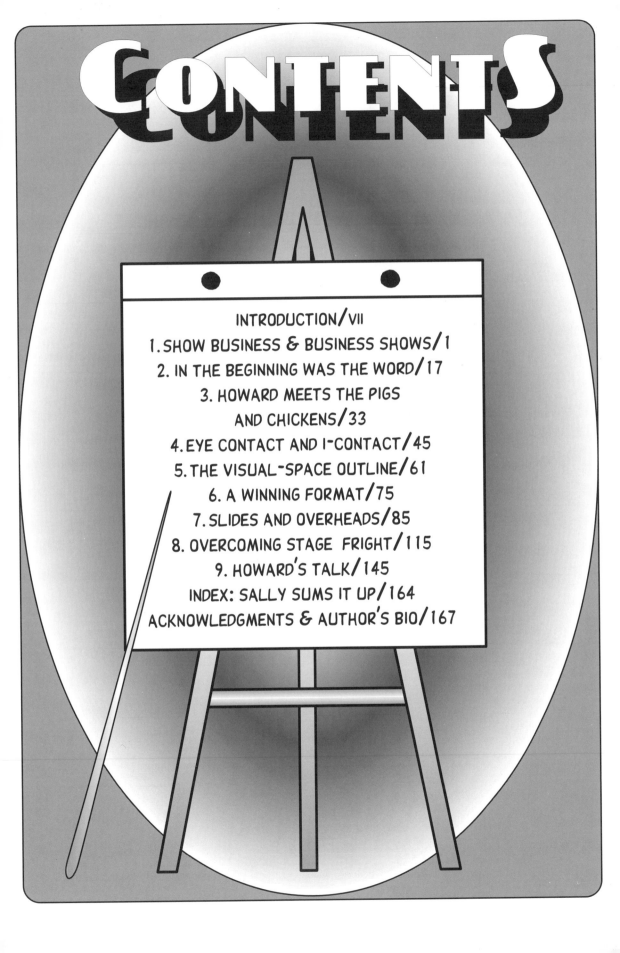

INTRODUCTION/VII

1. SHOW BUSINESS & BUSINESS SHOWS/1

2. IN THE BEGINNING WAS THE WORD/17

3. HOWARD MEETS THE PIGS
AND CHICKENS/33

4. EYE CONTACT AND I-CONTACT/45

5. THE VISUAL-SPACE OUTLINE/61

6. A WINNING FORMAT/75

7. SLIDES AND OVERHEADS/85

8. OVERCOMING STAGE FRIGHT/115

9. HOWARD'S TALK/145

INDEX: SALLY SUMS IT UP/164

ACKNOWLEDGMENTS & AUTHOR'S BIO/167

INTRODUCTION

I've never yet attended a public-speaking seminar where the instructor failed to mention the hoary old "fact" from the *Book of Lists*, that Americans fear public speaking more than death itself. I've never really believed it, either. As Seinfeld says, that means at a funeral we'd rather be the guy under the ground than the one giving the eulogy!

On the other hand, I sure know pre-talk anxiety well. In Chapter 8, "Overcoming Stage Fright," a fearful character reports that his head's shaking, his lips are dry, his hands are trembling, and his mind has gone blank. That was for me, the first time I had to speak in public. I was a student at Witwatersrand University in South Africa, and all I'd been asked to do was introduce a speaker. But I felt as though my mouth was filled with super glue and my head might fall off. Maybe, just at that point, death didn't seem so bad an option!

Much later in life, in Hawai'i, I gave a talk to another group. It was about as poor a performance as any speaker might offer, not because I was anxious or lacked the words, but because (I'm ashamed to admit) its content was completely inappropriate. I committed the greatest speaker's sin of all; not researching the audience. So I allowed myself to sound off, offended almost everyone, and in consequence lost out on some great professional opportunities.

In many ways, *Would You Really Rather Die Than Give a Talk?* comes out of those experiences. Some others, too. I've defeated my fear, worked hard on my public-speaking skills, and today make a living talking to groups of people, helping them become more effective communicators. Frankly, if *I* could overcome terror and tactlessness, anyone can.

Among the truths I've learned is that audiences love stories. So this book is largely presented as a narrative, with fictional characters in real-life situations. At its center is Howard Schwartz, a software engineer who has to make a presentation to an unfamiliar group. He's the one with the wobbly head and blank mind in Chapter 8, and you can bet too that he discovers the wisdom (and techniques) of audience analysis! His help and guide is Sally Browne, who is and is not me, a professional talk instructor who takes him through the process of organizing and delivering a winning presentation. We see Howard do it too, at the end of the book (Chapter 9).

Along the way we learn about the "showbiz" of showbiz shows (Chapter 1), how to use language effectively (Chapter 2), audience analysis (Chapter 3), effective openings and closings (Chapter 4), ways to organize material (Chapter 5), some original formatting strategies (Chapter 6), and the most up-to-date techniques of graphic design (Chapter 7).

This book is meant to be hands-on practical, useful, and informative. Its comic-book format allows you to see as well as read. And it is, hopefully, amusing and entertaining. By the end, I also hope, you'll much rather give a talk than embrace the sad alternative!

M.E.E.
May 1997

-5-

THE BEST WAY INTO THE *DYNAMIC PRESENTATIONS* SYSTEM IS TO START WITH YOURSELF! WHAT'S *YOUR* CURRENT LEVEL OF PRESENTATIONS COMPETENCE?

I BROUGHT ALONG THIS WORK SHEET TO HELP YOU FIND OUT! CIRCLE THE ANSWERS BELOW THAT BEST DESCRIBE YOU, THEN TOTAL UP!

A. Before making a presentation, do you:

Always   *Never*

1. Think about your audience, their expectations and knowledge-level of your subject?   5 4 3 2 1

2. Write down your objectives?   5 4 3 2 1

3. Research and take notes?   5 4 3 2 1

4. Know what action you want your audience to take?   5 4 3 2 1

5. Develop an outline?   5 4 3 2 1

6. Rehearse?   5 4 3 2 1

7. Anticipate questions and prepare your responses?   5 4 3 2 1

8. **Work out an attention-getting opener?**   5   4   3   2   1

9. **Check out the room, equipment and seating arrangements ahead of time?**   5   4   3   2   1

10. **Convert your pre-talk tension to force, drive and power?**   5   4   3   2   1

B. During your presentation, do you:

11. **Avoid reading your talk?**   5   4   3   2   1

12. **Use cue cards with compact notes?**   5   4   3   2   1

13. **Maintain eye-contact with your audience?**   5   4   3   2   1

14. **Move and gesture appropriately?**   5   4   3   2   1

15. **Consciously vary your vocal tone, volume and speed for emphasis?**   5   4   3   2   1

16. **Communicate enthusiastically?**   5   4   3   2   1

17. **Ensure that your audience understands the benefits to them of your proposals?**   5   4   3   2   1

18. **Use the word *You* as often as possible?**   5   4   3   2   1

19. **Use language that's relaxed and conversational, not stilted or formal?**   5   4   3   2   1

20. **Wind up with a punchy conclusion summarizing your case and the action you want your audience to take?**   5   4   3   2   1

TOTAL

WHAT
I WANT FROM THIS BOOK

☐ Cut my preparation time.

☐ Turn my pre-talk anxiety into drive and power.

☐ Deal easily with questions from the floor.

☐ Master powerful language use.

☐ Develop ways to organize my ideas into logical formats.

☐ Build self-confidence and dynamism.

☐ Learn to speak without notes.

☐ Design and use visual aids.

☐ Other:_____

_____

-16-

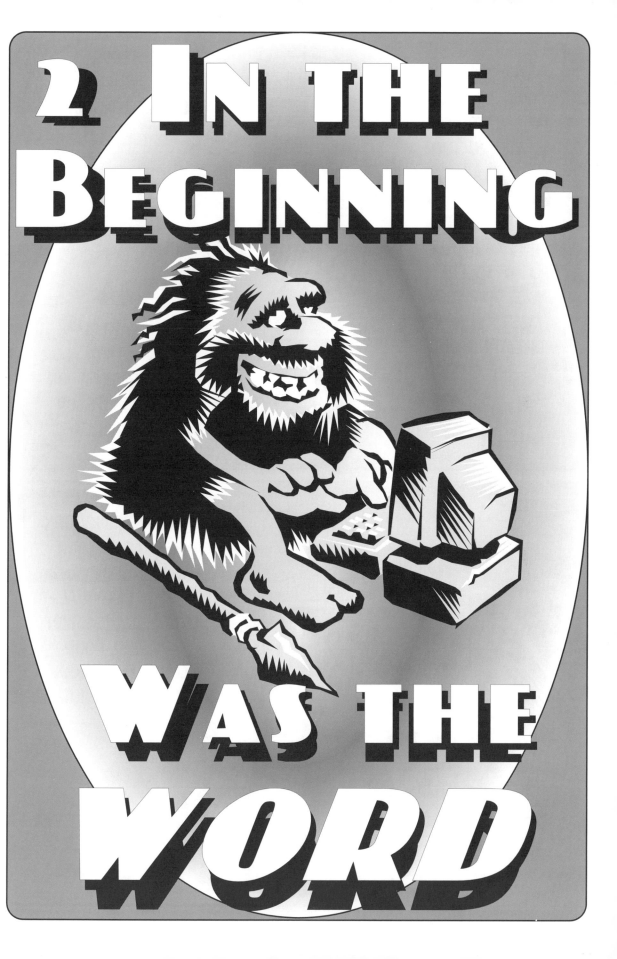

ONE WAY TO THINK OF YOUR PRESENTATION IS AS A STRUCTURE. YOU PLAN IT, GATHER ALL YOUR MATERIALS, AND THEN CAREFULLY PUT IT TOGETHER. NOTE THAT YOUR MOST COMMON OPERATING UNIT IS THE *WORD*.

WORDS ARE LIKE BRICKS! THEIR QUALITY, NATURE AND DESIGN...

...DETERMINE WHETHER YOUR PRESENTATION STANDS OR FALLS!

VERBAL BRICKWORK ALSO AFFECTS THE OVERALL LOOK...AND, LIKE A REAL REAL-ESTATE TRANSACTION, WHETHER YOUR CUSTOMERS DECIDE TO BUY OR NOT!

FOR SALE

-21-

THE IDEA EXTENDS BEYOND WAVES AND RAINBOWS! EDWARD SAPIR (1884-1939) ARGUED THAT LANGUAGES CONTAIN ASSUMPTIONS ABOUT THE WORLD THAT ARE SO "BUILT IN," NATIVE SPEAKERS DON'T EVEN NOTICE THE WAY THEIR PERCEPTIONS ARE BEING SHAPED!

WE SEE AND HEAR AND EXPERIENCE AS WE DO BECAUSE THE LANGUAGE HABITS OF OUR COMMUNITY PREDISPOSE CERTAIN CHOICES OF INTERPRETATION.*

*SAPIR: *LANGUAGE, CULTURE AND PERSONALITY*, P. 32.

MOST EUROPEAN LANGUAGES, FOR INSTANCE, "FACE" THE FUTURE AND "ADVANCE" OPTIMISTICALLY TOWARD IT.

YET OTHERS, LIKE ANGLO-SAXON, HAVE NO FUTURE TENSE. A FEW EVEN TRAVEL BACKWARD!

FOR THEIR SPEAKERS, THE PAST LIES ALL BEFORE, FULLY KNOWN, WHILE WHAT'S TO COME CAN BE GLIMPSED ONLY PARTIALLY OVER UNCERTAIN SHOULDERS!

THE THEORY OF EVOLUTION HINGES CRUCIALLY ON THE ASSUMPTION THAT SPECIES "ADVANCE" OVER TIME! IS THIS THOUGHT EVEN POSSIBLE IN A LANGUAGE THAT REVERSES INTO A DARK UNKNOWN?

WHORF: "A CHANGE IN LANGUAGE CAN TRANSFORM OUR APPRECIATION OF THE COSMOS ...EVEN EINSTEIN'S THEORY OF RELATIVITY HAS A BASIS IN THE FACT THAT INDO-EUROPEAN LANGUAGES USE MANY SPACE WORDS AND PATTERNS FOR DEALING WITH TIME."*

*WHORF: *LANGUAGE, THOUGHT AND REALITY*, PP. 263-266.

-25-

FAR BETTER TO FRAME YOUR PRESENTATION BY REDEFINING THE ISSUE IN A PRINCIPLED WAY: IN TERMS OF (SAY) THE NEED, COST, AVAILABILITY AND OVERALL FUNCTION AND PURPOSE OF COMPUTER SYSTEMS IN YOUR COMPANY.

STEP ONE: PRINCIPLED FRAMING

THE IDEA IS TO PHRASE THE TERMS OF THE DEBATE IN A WAY THAT "PREDISPOSES INTERPRETATION" TOWARD THE DECISION YOU PREFER!

THE CHOICE OF KEY WORDS IS CRUCIAL...

STEP ONE

THE CORNERSTONE. IF THIS IS GRANTED, THE REST FOLLOWS.

THESE DEDUCE LOGICALLY FROM CORNERSTONE DEFINITIONS.

STEP TWO

STEP TWO

CONCLUSION BASED ON STEPS ONE AND TWO.

STEP THREE

STEP THREE

STEP THREE

PARADIGM STRUCTURE FOR A THREE-LEVEL ARGUMENT.

EXCELLENT PROPOSAL!

VERY WELL ARGUED!

...GIVEN OUR OBJECTIVES, THEN, PENTIUM LAPTOPS ARE THE ONLY REAL OPTION!

AVOID THE POMPOSITY TRAP...
CHOOSE SHORT, EXPRESSIVE
WORDS AND SHORT, EXPRESSIVE
SENTENCES. SAID WINSTON
CHURCHILL, WHOSE ORATORY
WAS JUDGED TO BE WORTH
20 DIVISIONS TO BRITAIN
IN WORLD WAR TWO...

SMALL WORDS ARE BEST, AND THE OLD SMALL WORDS ARE BEST OF ALL!*

*BRENTWOOD SPEECH, 1957.

THEN USE THESE WORDS TO PAINT DRAMATIC VERBAL SCENES YOUR AUDIENCE CAN *SEE* IN THEIR MIND'S EYE! REMEMBER DALE CARNEGIE'S FAMOUS ADVICE: "PICTURES! PICTURES! PICTURES! SPRINKLE THEM THROUGH YOUR TALKS AND YOU'LL BE MORE INFLUENTIAL!"*

*THE QUICK AND EASY WAY TO EFFECTIVE SPEAKING, P. 81.

THE BEST WAY TO "TALK PICTURES" IS TO CONSTRUCT GRAPHIC, PAINTERLY COMPARISONS, SIMILES AND ANALOGIES, LIKE THE WORD *SPRINKLE*, ABOVE.

BUT BE BOLDER AND EVEN MORE ADVENTUROUS! MARTIN LUTHER KING'S, "I HAVE A DREAM!" SPEECH, THE MOST POWERFUL BY A MODERN AMERICAN, CONTAINS NO FEWER THAN 60 VIVID METAPHORS, MANY BUILT AROUND THE EMOTIVE OPPOSITIONS OF HEAT/THIRST/ INJUSTICE AND COOL/WATER/JUSTICE.

...A DESERT STATE SWELTERING IN THE HEAT OF INJUSTICE AND OPPRESSION WILL BE TRANSFORMED INTO AN OASIS OF FREEDOM AND JUSTICE!

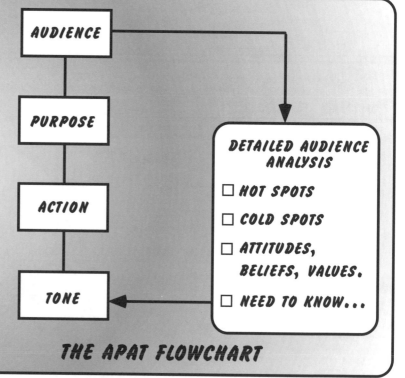

THE APAT FLOWCHART

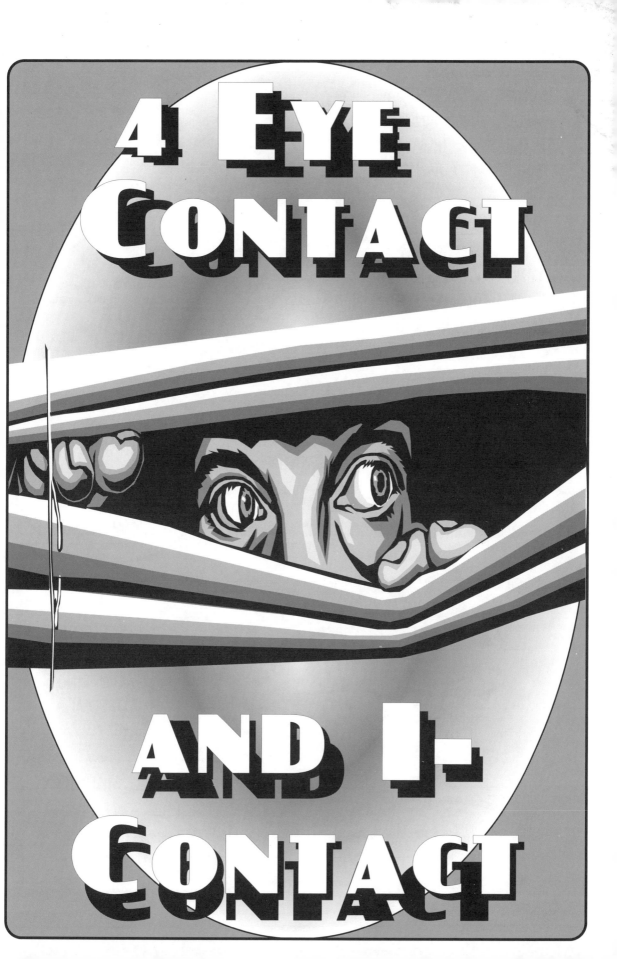

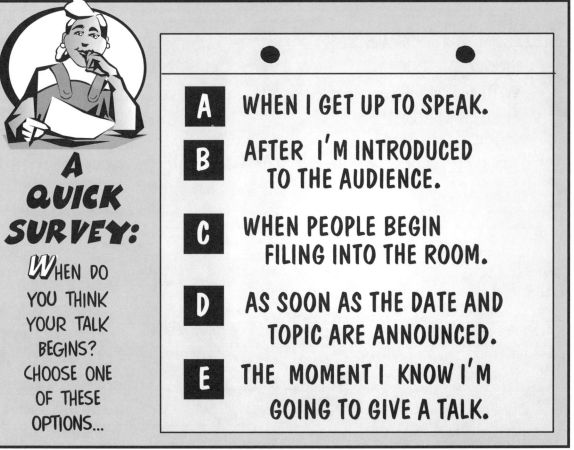

-48-

HEY! HE'S GOT A PH.D. AND 20 YEARS' EXPERIENCE!

SEND YOUR CONTACT A BRIEF DESCRIPTION OF YOUR TALK WITH A NOTE SAYING THEY'RE WELCOME TO USE IT IN ANY ANNOUNCEMENT. BE SURE TO INCLUDE YOUR QUALIFICATIONS.

THE BOARD'S GONNA LOVE THIS!

IF YOU'RE SPEAKING TO A GROUP YOU'VE NEVER MET BEFORE, MAKE SURE SOMEONE'S ASSIGNED TO INTRODUCE YOU. IF THEY HAVEN'T PICKED ANYONE FOR THIS TASK, POLITELY REQUEST THAT THEY DO.

NO PROBLEM, HOWARD! I'LL ASK MARGE BURR TO DO IT. SHE'S OUR COMMUNICATIONS PERSON!

-50-

-53-

NOTICE THAT QUOTES AND BUMPER STICKERS, ETC., CAN BE COLLECTED IN ADVANCE! MAKE A HABIT OF FILING MATERIAL YOU MIGHT BE ABLE TO USE LATER. I CALL IT MY SPEAKER'S ARMORY!

ANOTHER PRACTICAL RESOURCE IS THE *SPEAKER'S IDEA FILE,* A MONTHLY NEWSLETTER FROM RAGAN COMMUNICATIONS.* IT'S FULL OF QUOTES, ANECDOTES, HUMOR AND STATISTICS APPROPRIATE FOR BUSINESS PRESENTATIONS!

*THERE IS NO CONNECTION BETWEEN THE AUTHOR AND THIS CO.

8. TELL A STORY

WHEN ROBERT FULTON INVENTED THE STEAMBOAT, THE SKEPTICS YELLED: *"IT'LL NEVER START! IT'LL NEVER START!"* AFTER IT GOT GOING, THEY SHOUTED: *"IT'LL NEVER STOP! IT'LL NEVER STOP!"** SOME PEOPLE, YOU SEE, ARE NATURAL DOUBTERS--THEY'LL ALWAYS FIND A PROBLEM! NOW...

*SPEAKER'S IDEA FILE BROCHURE, P. 2.

9. PERSONAL ANECDOTE

I VIVIDLY REMEMBER LEARNING TO RIDE A BIKE. WHAT I DISCOVERED, OF COURSE, WAS THAT THE FASTER I PEDALED, THE EASIER IT WAS TO KEEP MY BALANCE. BUT THE FIRST TIME I PUSHED OFF HARD WAS AN ACT OF SHEER, MAD COURAGE! BUSINESS SUCCESS IS OFTEN LIKE THAT, TOO. YOU MIGHT HAVE TO TAKE A COUNTER-INTUITIVE GAMBLE, BUT...

A GREAT OPENING DESERVES AN EQUALLY SUCCESSFUL ENDING. EVERY GOOD SHOW BUILDS TOWARD A POWERFUL FINALE!

CRAFTING AN EFFECTIVE CLOSE IS ALMOST AS IMPORTANT AS YOUR START! A GOOD ENDING CEMENTS YOUR RELATIONSHIP WITH YOUR AUDIENCE AND PROVIDES THAT FINAL OPPORTUNITY TO DRIVE YOUR POINT HOME...LIKE A NAIL! HERE ARE FOUR SUGGESTIONS...!

THE FIRST AND MOST DYNAMIC IS CALLED THE ABC, OR ACTION-BENEFIT CONCLUSION!

YOU SIMPLY STATE CLEARLY THE ACTION YOU WOULD LIKE YOUR AUDIENCE TO TAKE, THEN SUM UP THE BENEFITS TO THEM IF THEY DO IT.

5 The Visual-Space Outline

-65-

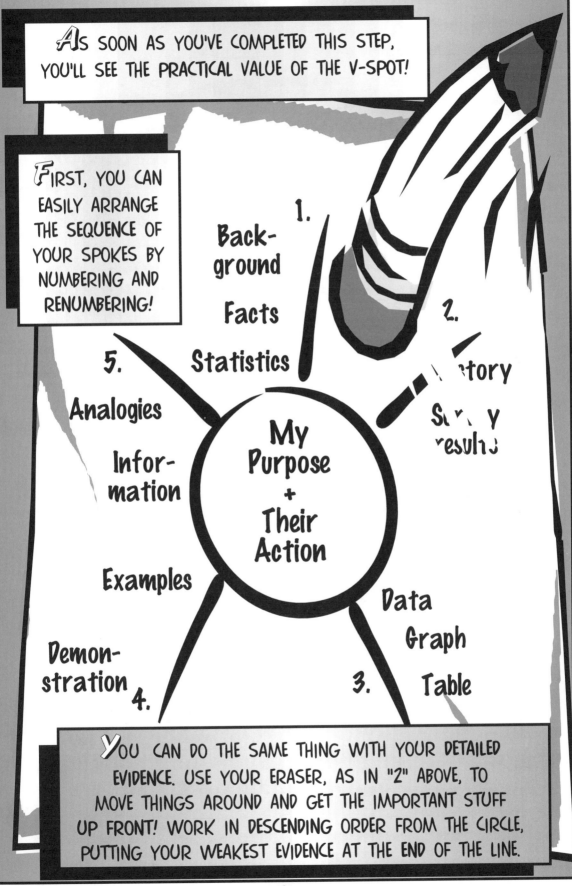

As soon as you've completed this step, you'll see the practical value of the V-SPOT!

First, you can easily arrange the sequence of your spokes by numbering and renumbering!

1.
Back-ground
Facts
Statistics

2.
story
Survey results

5.
Analogies
Infor-mation

My Purpose + Their Action

Examples

Data
Graph
Table
3.

Demon-stration
4.

You can do the same thing with your detailed evidence. Use your eraser, as in "2" above, to move things around and get the important stuff up front! Work in descending order from the circle, putting your weakest evidence at the end of the line.

ORG. CHART

CEO → VP → DEPT.

A TABLE IS ANY KIND OF GRAPHIC YOU USE TO SUM UP COMPLEX NUMERICAL OR OTHER DATA: A PIE CHART OR HOLOGRAM, TABULATED INFORMATION OR LINE GRAPH.

NOTE THAT *TABLES* ARE ALWAYS VISUAL. YOU CAN EITHER DRAW THEM ON YOUR FLIP CHART, OR PREPARE THEM IN ADVANCE AS SLIDES OR OVERHEADS. BUT *EXAMPLES, ANALOGIES, STATISTICS* AND *EXPERTS* ARE USUALLY VERBAL, AND INCLUDED IN THE SPOKEN TEXT OF YOUR PRESENTATION.

ANALOGY — EXAMPLE — STATISTICS — EXPERT

FOR INSTANCE, COMPARE TEN TRILLION TO THESE MITES, AS SIR JASPER SAYS!

AN EXAMPLE IS A SPECIFIC INSTANCE THAT ILLUSTRATES YOUR LARGER POINT. AUDIENCES LOVE THE HARD-EDGED FEEL OF A PARTICULAR CASE THEY CAN MENTALLY WALK AROUND AND WEIGH!

FOR EXAMPLE...

...A PROPOSAL FOR WORKER EMPOWERMENT AND OVERALL CULTURE CHANGE CAN BE MADE CONCRETE BY DESCRIBING THE CONSEQUENCES FOR A PARTICULAR INDIVIDUAL AND HIS/HER JOB! THE EXAMPLE MAKES THE LARGER IDEA REAL!

LEARNING TO USE THE INTERNET IS A BIT LIKE LEARNING TO RIDE A BIKE...BUT A WHOLE LOT SAFER!

ANALOGIES ARE USEFUL WHEN INTRODUCING IDEAS THAT MAY BE NOVEL OR UNFAMILIAR. YOU COMPARE WHAT'S UNKNOWN TO SOMETHING ALREADY WITHIN YOUR HEARERS' EXPERIENCE, NATURALIZING THE NEW AND GIVING IT A RECOGNIZABLE IDENTITY!

AS FOR STATISTICS...

...MARK TWAIN WAS ONLY HALF RIGHT WHEN HE JOKED THAT THERE ARE LIES, DAMN LIES, AND STATISTICS!

PRESENTED WITH INTEGRITY AND ACCURACY, NUMERICAL DATA CAN BE A POWERFUL SUPPORT!

EXPERTS ARE PEOPLE, LIKE MARK TWAIN, WHOSE REPUTATION, EXPERIENCE AND KNOWLEDGE GIVE THEIR OPINIONS AUTHORITY.

EXPERTS DON'T ALWAYS HAVE TO BE FAMOUS, SO LONG AS THEY'RE KNOWN AND RESPECTED BY YOUR AUDIENCE. YOU'LL KNOW WHO THEIR EXPERTS ARE BECAUSE OF YOUR FIRST STEP, AUDIENCE RESEARCH.

THE FINAL WEAPON IN YOUR SPEAKER'S ARMORY IS ALSO THE BIGGEST--DEMONSTRATION! THE OPPORTUNITY TO PHYSICALLY PERFORM A PROCESS--THAT IS, TO DO SOMETHING ON THE SPOT, IN REAL TIME--IS THE SINGLE GREATEST ADVANTAGE PUBLIC SPEAKING HAS OVER WRITING, TELEPHONES, FAX MACHINES OR E-MAIL!

YOUR FIRST CREATIVE THOUGHT, ONCE YOU KNOW YOU'LL BE GIVING A PRESENTATION, SHOULD BE: WHAT CAN I DEMONSTRATE? IN MOST CASES, YOU CAN SUCCESSFULLY BUILD YOUR TALK AROUND IT!

Safety Demonstration

LET ME SHOW YOU EXACTLY HOW SAFE OUR NEW PROCESS IS!

ANYCO BUSINESS PRESENTATION COMPANY

TELL ME & I'LL UNDERSTAND; SHOW ME AND I'LL NEVER FORGET!

ACTIONS ALWAYS SPEAK LOUDER THAN WORDS!

A GREAT DEMONSTRATION IS WHERE SHOW BUSINESS AND BUSINESS SHOWS CONNECT!

CENTRAL DEMO

STATISTICS

TABLES

EXPERTS

ANALOGIES

EXAMPLES

YOUR HOT-SPOT ANALYSIS WILL TELL YOU WHAT YOUR AUDIENCE IS LOOKING FOR! DRAMATIZE IT! BUILD AN ACTION AROUND IT!

THEN SUPPORT YOUR DEMO WITH THE OTHER T.E.A.S.E.D. OPTIONS! GIVE EACH NEW POINT ITS OWN UNIQUE FORM--A TABLE OR POWERFUL QUOTE FOR ONE, AN EXAMPLE OR FORCEFUL ANALOGY FOR ANOTHER, STATISTICS FOR A THIRD!

HOWARD, THE REASON THOSE OLD ROUTINES DON'T WORK ANYMORE IS THAT THEY WEREN'T DEVELOPED FOR BUSINESS PRESENTATIONS! INTRODUCTION, BODY AND CONCLUSION WAS INVENTED BY THE ANCIENT GREEKS OVER 2500 YEARS AGO!*

*ARISTOTLE: RHETORIC 3, 1371: 21-25.

TELL EM WHAT YOU'RE GOING TO SAY...SAY IT... TELL 'EM WHAT YOU SAID...GOES BACK TO THE FIFTIES. IT'S FAR TOO DULL AND LONG-WINDED FOR CONTEMPORARY AUDIENCES EXPECTING TO BE ENTERTAINED, AMUSED AND INFORMED!

WHAT YOU NEED IS A FORMAT THAT'S AS SLICK AS TV, PLOTTED LIKE AN ADVENTURE MOVIE, AND COMPELLING AS AN AD CAMPAIGN! YOU NEED THE WIN-STORY FORMAT!

THE WIN-STORY FORMAT?

YES! THE VERSATILE WIN-STORY FORMAT GIVES LIFE, FORCE, POWER AND DRAMA TO ANY BUSINESS TALK.

BUT HERE'S OUR FOOD! I'LL TELL YOU ABOUT IT AS WE EAT!

6 A WINNING FORMAT

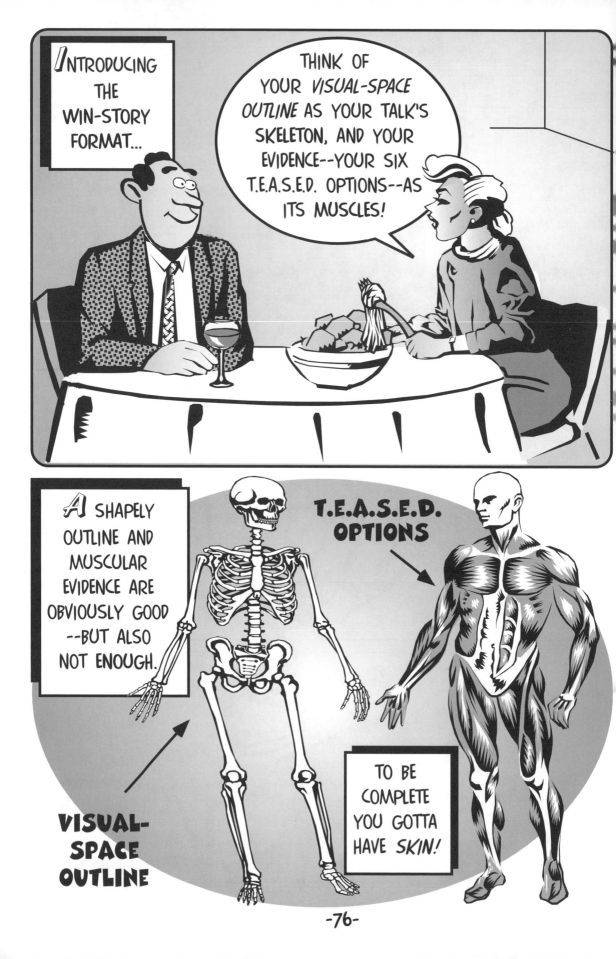

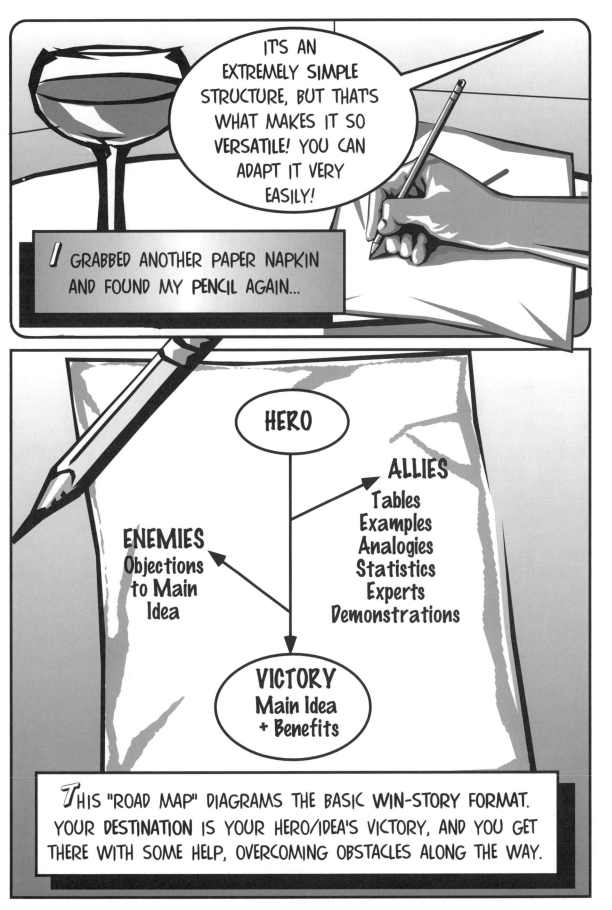

PRESENTATIONS ARE BUSINESS TALKS ILLUSTRATED WITH GRAPHICS--SLIDES, OVERHEADS, FLIP CHARTS. HOW YOU DESIGN AND USE THEM CAN MAKE OR MAR YOUR SUCCESS!

"Do unto others before they do unto you!"
--Anon

THE MAIN FUNCTION OF A GRAPHIC IS TO PROVIDE VISUAL PUNCTUATION TO WHAT YOU'RE SAYING AT THE TIME! IT CAN BE A GRAPH, A CHART, A PICTURE OR EVEN A STRIKING QUOTE!

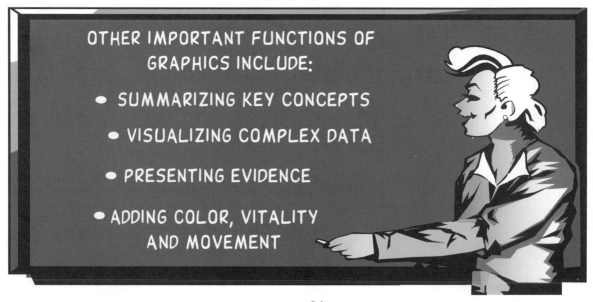

OTHER IMPORTANT FUNCTIONS OF GRAPHICS INCLUDE:

- SUMMARIZING KEY CONCEPTS
- VISUALIZING COMPLEX DATA
- PRESENTING EVIDENCE
- ADDING COLOR, VITALITY AND MOVEMENT

KEEP IN MIND THAT YOUR VISUALS ARE AN INTEGRAL PART OF THE SHOW--IN FACT, THEIR LOOK, HANDLING AND TIMING SHOULD BE PURE SHOW BUSINESS ALL THE WAY!

BA-BA-BOOM!

PRESE NOW!

E-Z GRAFIX

OVERHEADS IN OVERTIME

FOR THESE AND OTHER REASONS, WE RECOMMEND NOT USING COMMERCIAL PRESENTATIONS SOFTWARE...THEY'RE FAST AND EASY, BUT ALSO BLAND AND HOMOGENEOUS. UNLESS YOU'RE IN A REAL HURRY, AVOID THEM. *YOU CAN DO MUCH BETTER DESIGNING YOUR OWN!*

OUR ADVICE IS THAT YOU LIMIT YOURSELF TO JUST A FEW EXCELLENT OVERHEADS OR SLIDES DRAMATIZING YOUR MAIN POINTS. FOR AN HOUR'S TALK THAT SHOULD BE NO MORE THAN SIX! THE RULE IS: *ONE HOUR, SIX POINTS, SIX GRAPHICS!*

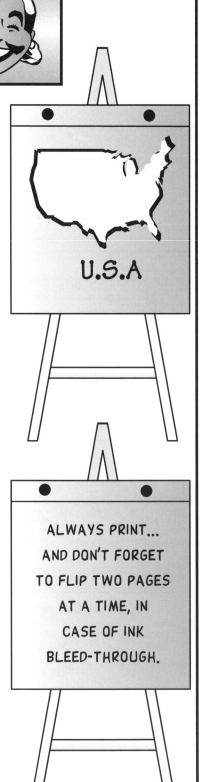

HERE ARE SOME MORE FLIP CHART TIPS...

LIGHTLY DRAW YOUR GRAPHIC AHEAD OF TIME, JUST ENOUGH SO ONLY YOU CAN SEE IT...THEN BOLDLY INK IT IN WHILE TALKING! THE EFFECT WILL BE DRAMATIC--LIKE A CONJURING TRICK!! NOW THAT'S WHAT I CALL SHOWBIZ!

U.S.A

U.S.A

FAINTLY PENCIL IN SOME NOTES FOR YOURSELF. IMPRESS YOUR LISTENERS WITH YOUR MEMORY AND COMMAND OF DETAIL.

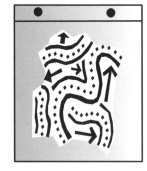

COMPLEX GRAPHICS OR LONG LISTS SHOULD BE DONE IN ADVANCE, JUST LIKE SLIDES OR OVERHEADS. AS YOUR TALK PROCEEDS, YOU FLIP MASTERFULLY FROM PAGE TO PAGE!

ALWAYS PRINT... AND DON'T FORGET TO FLIP TWO PAGES AT A TIME, IN CASE OF INK BLEED-THROUGH.

THE JAPANESE MARKET TODAY

*R*EALLY BIG AUDIENCES, 150 AND UP, CAN HANDLE VIDEOS PROJECTED ON A LARGE SCREEN. CATALOGS LIST A HUGE SELECTION OF BUSINESS-ORIENTED MATERIAL.

*U*NLESS YOU'RE EXPERIENCED, DON'T TRY TO SHOOT YOUR OWN! AMATEUR VIDEOS TEND TO BE POOR AND EMBARRASSING.

VERY SMALL GROUPS--5 OR 6--MIGHT APPRECIATE A MULTIMEDIA PRESENTATION ON YOUR LAPTOP, FOLLOWED BY A Q-&-A SESSION.

BUT REMEMBER: THE MORE ELABORATE YOUR MEDIA, THE LESS YOU'LL BE SEEN!

A TYPICAL BUSINESS AUDIENCE IS 20-25 PEOPLE. FOR THESE GROUPS, PREPARE OVERHEADS. THEY'RE MORE VERSATILE AND EASIER TO USE THAN SLIDES, AND WITH MODERN COLOR PRINTERS AND XEROXING, ARE A SNAP TO CUSTOMIZE!

FORTUNATELY, THERE IS A MIDDLE GROUND BETWEEN THE JOYLESS FUNCTIONALISM OF THE VIENNA SCHOOL AND THE EXCESSIVE EXUBERANCE OF MODERN MAGAZINE GRAPHICS!

IT'S BEST REPRESENTED BY DR. EDWARD R. TUFTE, WHO TEACHES GRAPHIC DESIGN, STATISTICS AND POLITICAL ECONOMY AT YALE.*

*T*UFTE HAS WRITTEN TWO FAMOUS BOOKS ON THE SUBJECT: *ENVISIONING INFORMATION* (1990) AND *THE VISUAL DISPLAY OF QUANTITATIVE INFORMATION* (1983). THEY HAVE WON OVER TEN PRIZES FOR DESIGN AND CONTENT. TUFTE HIMSELF IS A MEMBER OF FOUR PRESTIGIOUS PROFESSIONAL ASSOCIATIONS, AND HAS ADVISED ON STATISTICS AND GRAPHICS FOR *THE NEW YORK TIMES, NEWSWEEK,* CBS, NBC, AND THE BUREAU OF CENSUS.

*PRONOUNCED *TUFTY*. ALL QUOTES IN THE FOLLOWING IMAGINARY INTERVIEW ARE BASED ON TUFTE'S BOOKS AND ARTICLES, USING HIS OWN WORDS AND EXAMPLES WHEREVER POSSIBLE.

LET ME SHOW YOU AN EXAMPLE. IT MAY WELL BE THE BEST STATISTICAL GRAPHIC EVER DRAWN!

IT WAS CREATED IN 1861 BY CHARLES J. MINARD TO DEPICT THE TERRIBLE FATE OF NAPOLEON'S RUSSIAN CAMPAIGN IN 1812-1813.

THE VISUAL DISPLAY OF QUANTITATIVE INFORMATION, PP. 40-41.

"LEFT TO RIGHT, THE SHRINKING **UPPER** BAND SHOWS THE ARMY'S LOSSES AS IT MOVED ACROSS RUSSIA, IN THE SUMMER OF 1812. OF 422,000 MEN, BARELY 100,000 REACHED MOSCOW. THEIR DEVASTATING WINTER RETREAT IS MARKED BY THE DARK LOWER BAND, LINKED TO A TEMPERATURE SCALE AND DATES. ONLY 10,000 FINALLY MADE IT BACK INTO POLAND."

"IT HAS BEEN SAID THAT MINARD'S BRUTAL ELOQUENCE DEFIES THE PEN OF THE HISTORIAN! HE TELLS A RICH, COHERENT STORY, USING MULTIVARIATE DATA--MEANING THAT MANY VARIABLES ARE SIMULTANEOUSLY PLOTTED, INCLUDING...

...THE ARMY'S SIZE, LOCATION AND DIRECTION, AND THE GROWING COLD ON KNOWN DAYS DURING THE RETREAT."

EACH DETAIL ADDS SIGNIFICANCE TO THE OTHERS, AND DERIVES FURTHER MEANING FROM THEM!

EXACTLY! THE VISUAL TASK IS CONTRAST, COMPARISON AND CHOICE, SO THE MORE RELEVANT INFORMATION WITHIN EYESPAN, THE BETTER!

BUT I WAS TAUGHT DATA SHOULD BE BOILED DOWN AND SIMPLIFIED!

NO, THE QUANTITY OF DETAIL IS AN ISSUE COMPLETELY SEPARATE FROM THE DIFFICULTY OF READING! CLUTTER AND CONFUSION ARE FAILURES OF DESIGN, NOT ATTRIBUTES OF INFORMATION.

THE VISUAL DISPLAY OF QUANTITAVE INFORMATION, P. 40.
ENVISIONING INFORMATION, PP. 50-51.

THE VISUAL DISPLAY OF QUANTITATIVE INFORMATION, PP. 110-111.

*O*THER EXAMPLES OF CHARTJUNK INCLUDE HEAVILY-LINED GRIDS THAT OVERWHELM THE THE DATA. IN THE EXAMPLE BELOW, NOTE HOW MUCH CLEARER THE INFORMATION BECOMES AFTER THE GRID IS REMOVED!

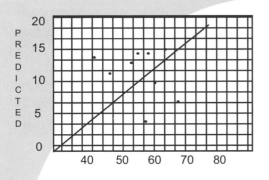

FAKE PERSPECTIVE IS SIMPLY MORE NOISE DROWNING OUT THE DATA.

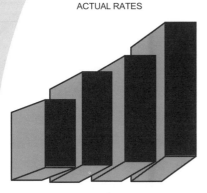

REDUNDANCY--IN THIS EXAMPLE, THE SAME DATA ARE GIVEN SIX DIFFERENT WAYS: HEIGHTS OF THE LEFT LINE, RIGHT LINE AND SHADING; POSITIONS OF THE TOP HORIZONTAL LINE AND THE NUMBER; AND THE NUMBER ITSELF!

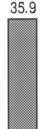

35.9

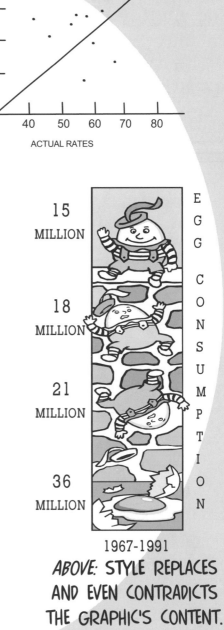

EGG CONSUMPTION

15 MILLION

18 MILLION

21 MILLION

36 MILLION

1967-1991

ABOVE: STYLE REPLACES AND EVEN CONTRADICTS THE GRAPHIC'S CONTENT.

THE VISUAL DISPLAY OF QUANTITATIVE INFORMATION, PP. 80, 94, 96, 112, 118.

"ONE OF THE WORST CONSEQUENCES OF CHARTJUNK IS LYING BY VISUAL EXAGGERATION. IN THIS EXAMPLE, THE RELATIVE BARREL SIZES IMPLY A PRICE INCREASE OF 27,000 PERCENT INSTEAD OF THE ACTUAL 454 PERCENT! ALSO, IN THE FOUR YEARS PRIOR TO 1979, THE REAL PRICE OF OIL ACTUALLY DECLINED.

"BUSY WITH DECORATION, THE GRAPHIC MISSED THE NEWS!"

THE VISUAL DISPLAY OF QUANTITATIVE INFORMATION, PP. 62, 71.

IN THE BARREL...

Price per bbl. of light crude, leaving Saudi Arabia on Jan. 1

April 1 $14.55

$13.34

$12.70

$12.09

$11.51

$10.46

$10.95

$2.41

'73 '74 '75 '76 1977 1978 1979

POINT WELL TAKEN! NOW, WHAT ABOUT COLOR...ANY, UM, BRIGHT IDEAS!?

ACTUALLY, DON'T OVERDO THE BRIGHT COLORS OR YOU MIGHT END UP WITH COLOR-JUNK! GO FOR LIGHTER SHADES--BLUES, YELLOWS AND GRAYS!

COLOR CAN OF COURSE BE PLEASANTLY DECORATIVE, BUT IN GRAPHICS IT'S BEST USED TO MEASURE, LABEL AND REPRESENT REALITY (SUCH AS A BLUE SEA).

ENVISIONING INFORMATION, PP. 81-82, 90.

EDWARD TUFTE'S PRINCIPLES OF GRAPHICAL DESIGN

1. AT THE HEART OF QUANTITATIVE REASONING IS A SINGLE QUESTION: *COMPARED TO WHAT?*

2. BECAUSE OF THIS, GRAPHICAL EXCELLENCE REQUIRES TELLING THE TRUTH, AND IS NEARLY ALWAYS MULTIVARIATE.

3. GOOD GRAPHICS GIVE THE VIEWER THE GREATEST NUMBER OF IDEAS IN THE SHORTEST TIME WITH THE LEAST INK IN THE SMALLEST SPACE.

4. THEY SHOW DATA VARIATION, NOT DESIGN VARIATION. DESIGN VARIATION FOR ITS OWN SAKE IS CHARTJUNK.

5. LIKE MINARD'S CLASSIC, GOOD GRAPHICS OFTEN HAVE A NARRATIVE QUALITY, A STORY TO TELL ABOUT THE DATA.

6. IN SUM: CREATE SELF-EFFACING DISPLAYS INTENSELY COMMITTED TO RICH DATA.

THESE ARE KEY RECOMMENDATIONS, BUT THEY'RE ONLY A FEW OF THE MANY POINTS MADE IN MY BOOKS! INTERESTED READERS SHOULD CHECK THE FULL TEXTS!

ENVISIONING INFORMATION, PP. 35, 67.

THE VISUAL DISPLAY OF QUANTITATIVE INFORMATION, PP. 51, 77, 105, 176.

TUFTE'S WORK IS PARTICULARLY USEFUL WHEN IT COMES TO VISUALLY DISPLAYING NUMBERS. BUT WHAT ABOUT THE PRINCIPLES GOVERNING TEXT-BASED INFORMATION?

HERE ARE OUR SUGGESTIONS. I'M ASSUMING THAT YOU'LL BE WORKING WITH A DRAW PROGRAM ON A COMPUTER AND PRINTING OUT YOUR WORK ON A LASER OR INK-JET PRINTER.

EFFECTIVE GRAPHICS COMBINE WORDS AND PICTURES. THE RULE IS, *WORDS FIRST, PICTURES SECOND!*

GRAPHIC DESIGN

TOO MUCH PICTURE LOSES THE MESSAGE...

GRAPHIC DESIGN

1. But too much message, like this, should also be avoided. It's visually uninteresting, hard to read, and much too complex.

2. The font is too small, unimaginative and unvaried! People at the back won't be able to read it. Nor will they want to.

3. Wordy! There's far too much irrelevant verbal information. Good graphics work in headlines.

4. The dull format provides no guideposts or signs of emphasis to help the viewer assimilate the information.

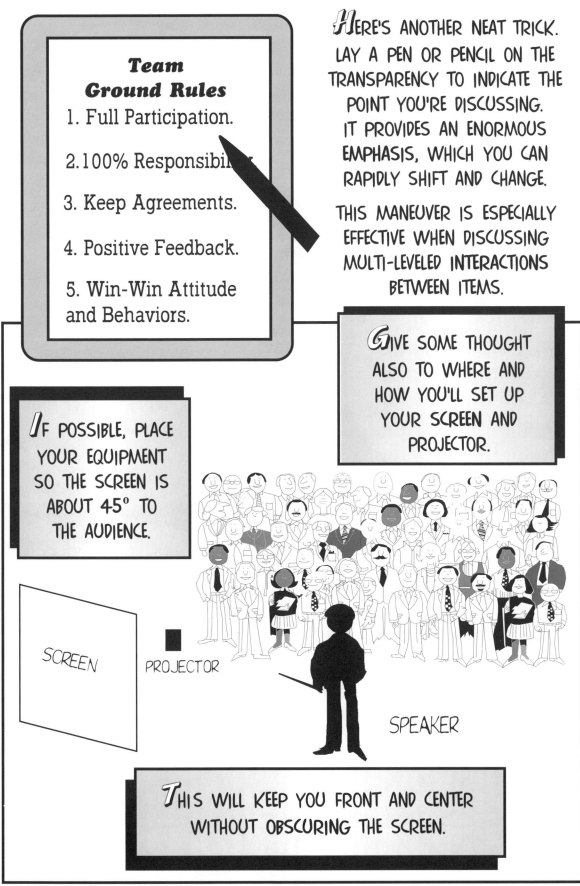

Team Ground Rules

1. Full Participation.

2. 100% Responsibility.

3. Keep Agreements.

4. Positive Feedback.

5. Win-Win Attitude and Behaviors.

HERE'S ANOTHER NEAT TRICK. LAY A PEN OR PENCIL ON THE TRANSPARENCY TO INDICATE THE POINT YOU'RE DISCUSSING. IT PROVIDES AN ENORMOUS EMPHASIS, WHICH YOU CAN RAPIDLY SHIFT AND CHANGE.

THIS MANEUVER IS ESPECIALLY EFFECTIVE WHEN DISCUSSING MULTI-LEVELED INTERACTIONS BETWEEN ITEMS.

GIVE SOME THOUGHT ALSO TO WHERE AND HOW YOU'LL SET UP YOUR SCREEN AND PROJECTOR.

IF POSSIBLE, PLACE YOUR EQUIPMENT SO THE SCREEN IS ABOUT 45° TO THE AUDIENCE.

SCREEN

PROJECTOR

SPEAKER

THIS WILL KEEP YOU FRONT AND CENTER WITHOUT OBSCURING THE SCREEN.

8 Overcoming Stage Fright

HOWARD WAS WAITING FOR ME WHEN I ARRIVED! AS SOON AS WE WERE ALONE HE SAID:
SALLY, I'M TERRIFIED! YOU WANNA KNOW WHY?? BECAUSE THIS THING'S GONNA BE A CATTLE MARKET AND I'M THE SACRIFICIAL COW! FOUR OTHER COMPANIES ARE MAKING PRESENTATIONS ON THE SAME DAY! I'VE HEARD THAT BILL BATES FROM MACROSOFT HIMSELF WILL BE THERE! PLUS THE TOP SALES EXECS FROM MARVELL, BYRON, AND SOFLINC! I CAN JUST SEE THEIR LASER POINTERS AND MULTI-MEDIA THINKPADS NOW! SALLY, I'M DEAD, I'M DEAD, I'M DEAD!

I'VE TRIED REHEARSING MY TALK...
...BUT I JUST FREEZE!
MY HEAD SHAKES LIKE IT'S SET ON A SPRING!
MY LIPS GUM UP...MY HANDS TREMBLE!
AND MY MIND...
...GOES... GOES...
BLANK!
AARGH!!

HOWARD, YOU'VE GOT A CLASSIC CASE OF STAGE FRIGHT!

S-STAGE FRIGHT?

YEP, PERFORMANCE ANXIETY. TAKE HEART, MY FRIEND, IT'S EXTREMELY COMMON...

OVER-COMING STAGE FRIGHT

...EVEN AMONG PEOPLE WHO'VE BEEN ON THE STAGE OR SPEAKER'S PLATFORM ALL THEIR LIVES!

THE MOST FAMOUS EXAMPLE IS SIR LAURENCE OLIVIER, WHO WAS SUDDENLY AFFLICTED WITH IT AFTER 50 YEARS ON THE STAGE!

"My courage sank... I began to watch for the instant at which my knowledge of the next line would vanish...

My voice started to fade, my throat closed up...the condition persisted and continued to torment me for five whole years."*

*LAURENCE OLIVIER: *CONFESSIONS OF AN ACTOR,* PP. 261-262.

-118-

-119-

BUT ALMOST THE FIRST THING YOU EVER TAUGHT ME ABOUT PUBLIC SPEAKING WAS NOT TO READ MY TALK ALOUD!

THAT'S RIGHT! GOOD PRESENTERS NEVER READ, YET THEY'RE FLUENT, ORGANIZED AND CONFIDENT! THEY APPEAR TO SPEAK SPONTANEOUSLY, YET KNOW EXACTLY WHAT COMES NEXT!

IN A COMPLEX PRESENTATION LIKE YOURS, THERE IS ONLY ONE WAY TO DO IT: *HAVE NOTES YOU CAN CONSULT AS NEEDED.*

HERE ARE SOME IDEAS. CHOOSE THE SYSTEM THAT SUITS YOU BEST!

*T*HE TRADITIONAL WAY IS TO PREPARE A CUE SHEET--USUALLY A 4"X5" INDEX CARD-- ON WHICH YOU WRITE A POINT-BY-POINT SUMMARY OF YOUR PRESENTATION.

Graphics
First principles
(a) Economy
(b) 4 pts. max
(c) 6 words/pt
(d) 7... xt

*S*IMPLY REFER TO IT AS YOU GO ALONG AND YOU'LL **NEVER** LOSE YOUR PLACE OR FORGET YOUR LINES! THAT'S A LUXURY OLIVIER NEVER HAD!

*B*ASE YOUR CUE-CARD SUMMARY ON YOUR VISUAL-SPACE OUTLINE. DEVELOP YOUR HEADINGS, SUB-HEADS AND EXAMPLES FROM YOUR TALK'S ORGANIZATIONAL PLAN.

*R*EMEMBER THAT YOU CAN ALWAYS USE MORE THAN ONE CUE CARD-- IN FACT, IT'S A GOOD IDEA TO DO SO IF YOU'RE INTENDING TO COVER A LOT OF TERRITORY. TAKE CARE TO NAME AND **NUMBER** THEM SO YOU ALWAYS KNOW WHERE YOU ARE.

VISUAL-SPACE OUTLINE

CUE CARDS WORK FINE, BUT FRANKLY THEY'RE OUT-DATED AND ALWAYS REMIND YOUR AUDIENCE THAT YOU'RE WORKING FROM A SCRIPT.

IT'S FAR BETTER TO HIDE YOUR NOTES SO ONLY YOU KNOW THEY'RE THERE!

YES, THAT'S RIGHT! I'M GOING TO SHOW YOU A MEMORY SYSTEM THAT WILL HELP YOU TO REMEMBER YOUR NOTES!
INSTEAD OF READING THEM OFF YOUR OVERHEAD, READ THEM OFF YOUR INNER HEAD!
BASED ON THE CONCEPT OF MEMORY HOOKS AND WORD ASSOCIATION, MY TECHNIQUE BUILDS ON THE MOST UP-TO-DATE RESEARCH ABOUT HOW PEOPLE RECALL AND MEMORIZE!
Browne & Co
Communications

HERE'S HOW THE SYSTEM WORKS. FIRST, WE CREATE A SHARP MENTAL PICTURE. READ THE DESCRIPTION IN THE NEXT BOX AND FIX THE IMAGE IN YOUR MIND.

THE SUN RISES INTO A CLEAR BLUE SKY AND SHINES UPON A TREE STANDING NEAR THE DOOR OF A QUAINT COTTAGE. A BEEHIVE HANGS FROM THE BRANCHES. BELOW IT ON THE GROUND IS A PILE OF STICKS!

OKAY, YOU ARE, UM, RATHER STATIC. WHAT ARE YOU GOING TO DO?

WELL...I GUESS I COULD MOVE AROUND A BIT AND GESTURE MORE.

*A*BSOLUTELY--*MOVEMENT* AND *GESTURE!* DON'T BE AFRAID TO USE THE FULL STAGE! GET OUT FROM BEHIND THAT PODIUM... ESPECIALLY AS YOU'VE GOT MOST OF YOUR NOTES IN YOUR HEAD!

*N*OTHING IS MORE EFFECTIVE THAN MOVING TOWARD YOUR AUDIENCE AS YOU SPEAK... REMEMBER ELIZABETH DOLE AT THE 1996 REPUBLICAN CONVENTION? CLINTON ALSO WON POINTS WHEN HE DID IT IN ONE OF HIS DEBATES WITH BUSH!

*B*UT USE IT SPARINGLY, AND BE SURE NOT TO GET TOO CLOSE OR THE AUDIENCE MAY FEEL YOU'RE INVADING THEIR SPACE! YOU JUST KINDA AMBLE FORWARD, LIKE YOU'RE TAKING THEM INTO YOUR CONFIDENCE!

GESTURES ARE INSEPARABLE FROM MEANING. THEY'RE AS IMPORTANT AS YOUR TONE, VOLUME, PACING AND EVEN INDIVIDUAL WORD SELECTION. SHAKESPEARE NOTED:

*HAMLET, III.II.5-15.

SUIT THE ACTION TO THE WORD, THE WORD TO THE ACTION...DO NOT SAW THE AIR TOO MUCH WITH YOUR HAND...BE NOT TOO TAME NEITHER, BUT LET YOUR DISCRETION BE YOUR TUTOR.*

THERE ARE TWO KINDS OF GESTURE: HABITUAL AND DELIBERATE. NOTICE THAT BOTH ARE LEARNED. IF YOU DON'T LIKE YOUR GESTURES, REDESIGN AND RELEARN THEM.!

HABITUAL GESTURES INCLUDE POSTURE, UNCONSCIOUS HAND AND FOOT ACTIONS, HEAD MOVEMENTS, ETC.

DELIBERATE GESTURES ARE THOSE YOU'VE PLANNED, LIKE A LAWYER DRAMATICALLY POINTING TO THE ACCUSED.

FINALLY, HOWARD, YOU SHOULD PLAN THE WAY YOU INTEND TO HANDLE QUESTIONS AT THE END.

BUT HOW CAN I DO THAT? I CAN'T ANTICIPATE SOMEONE'S QUERY!

SURE YOU CAN! THINK OF THE TWO OR THREE MOST DIFFICULT OR AWKWARD QUESTIONS YOU COULD BE ASKED. THEN WRITE DOWN YOUR ANSWERS ON A CUE CARD...JUST IN CASE!

QUESTION: "We never heard of you but we sure have heard of Macrosoft. So why shd we buy from you instead of them?"
- NEW COMPANY
- NEW PARADIGM
- NEWER TECHNOLOGY
- NEW IDEAS
- NEW APPROACH!

THE MOST IMPORTANT THING IN A Q&A SESSION IS MAKING SURE YOU KEEP CONTROL.

WHAT YOU DON'T WANT IS PEOPLE JUST THROWING QUESTIONS AT YOU, OR GETTING SUCKED INTO A LONG EXCHANGE WITH ONE PERSON!

BEAR IN MIND THAT IN A Q&A SESSION THE MOOD CHANGES: YOUR AUDIENCE MOVES FROM PASSIVE TO ACTIVE.

THE BEST WAY TO MAINTAIN CONTROL IS TO MODEL THE BEHAVIOR YOU WANT.

SOON AS YOU'RE DONE WITH YOUR MAIN SPEECH, STEP FORWARD, RAISE YOUR HAND, AND SAY: "ANY QUESTIONS OR COMMENTS?" KEEP YOUR HAND RAISED FOR A FEW SECONDS.

NOW AUDIENCE MEMBERS WILL RAISE THEIR OWN HANDS BEFORE SPEAKING AND WAIT FOR YOU TO SELECT THE QUESTIONER.

9

HOWARD'S TALK

CONDOR
L'EXPRESS

-151-

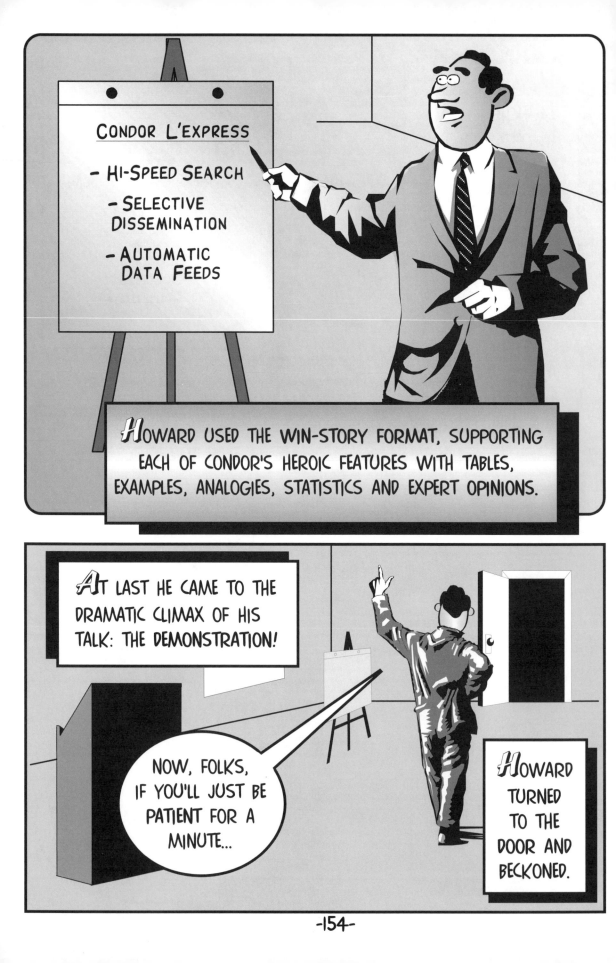

-154-

-156-

-158-

ON THE WAY HOME, HOWARD STARTED OBSESSING ABOUT HIS PERFORMANCE, SO I TAUGHT HIM THE SPEAKER'S FINAL LESSON...

DID I HANG BEHIND THE PODIUM TOO MUCH? MAYBE I SHOULD'VE EXPLAINED SCALABILITY MORE...DID YOU NOTICE I NEARLY DROPPED THE BOX?

HOWARD, THERE'S ONLY ONE USEFUL THING TO DO RIGHT NOW, AND THAT'S LEARN FROM THIS! NEXT TIME YOU'LL BE THAT MUCH BETTER!

ABOUT TWO WEEKS LATER, HE SENT ME AN E-MAIL...

Hello, Sally,

Guess what? That's right! I got the contract, and it was all thanks to you. Muchas gracias! If I can ever return the favor, you know you can count on me.

Oh, and guess what else? I got a call from none other than Bill Bates himself! He called to congratulate me. Said he heard I did a great job, etc. I told him I owed it all to you and he was very complimentary.

Thanks again,

Howard

DEMONSTRATIONS ARE WHERE SHOW BUSINESS AND BUSINESS SHOWS INTERSECT. WORK ON YOUR SHOWBIZ SKILLS! LEARN TO MEMORIZE YOUR NOTES, MOVE AND GESTURE EASILY, AND VARY YOUR VOICE.

PP. 6-9, 72-73, 123-139

GOOD PERFORMANCES START AND END WELL. CHOOSE AN ATTENTION-GRABBING OPENING AND A CONCLUSION THAT'S APPROPRIATE FOR YOUR AUDIENCE, PURPOSE, ACTION AND TONE!

PP. 52-60

AN EFFECTIVE TECHNIQUE IS TO FRAME YOUR TALK AS AN EXCITING DRAMA USING THE WIN-STORY FORMAT: *HERO* (MAIN IDEA), *ALLIES* (T.E.A.S.E.D. OPTIONS), *ENEMIES* (DEFEATED), *VICTORY* (ACTION-BENEFIT CONCLUSION).

PP. 80-84

BE CONSISTENT IN YOUR DESIGN FROM GRAPHIC TO GRAPHIC!

WHITE SPACE
PICTURES
• BULLETS
NO MORE THAN TWO FONTS

WHITE SPACE RELIEVES THE EYE!

Graphic Design-2
Basics of Visual Attractiveness

DESIGN YOUR GRAPHICS WITH BOLD SIMPLICITY. COMBINE WORDS AND PICTURES, BUT NEVER SACRIFICE YOUR DATA TO THE IMAGE.

PP. 96-114

AND FINALLY... *GO GET 'EM, TIGER!*

ALWAYS PREPARE FOR QUESTIONS...

PP. 140-143

Michael Egan
Spring, 1997